Untold Truths

Angelina Mateus

Angelina
Mateus

Untold Truths

Angelina Mateus

Copyright © 2023 Angelina Mateus
All rights reserved
ISBN: 9798372214071

DEDICATION

This book is dedicated to myself
for overcoming all the
obstacles life threw my way

ACKNOWLEDGMENTS

To Andrew Katz
For believing in my writing and being my mentor throughout this process

To Jesse James
For the beautiful artwork

To my loved ones
For pushing me to write this book

To myself
For being fierce despite everything I have been through

When walking she blooms
Flowers to leave her beauty behind

Angelina Mateus

With the intention
Of being deciphered
Fragments of my heart
Are being unleashed
Into significant poems

In some way or another
Poetry is in all of us
You become a poem
When you turn into
The poet's muse

Unfazed by obstacles ahead
Waves are constantly
Dancing to the motion of life
All they do
Is change their rhythmic dance
Swaying away to different beats
To keep afloat in this world

You need to acknowledge
Life is only lived once
Every day is an opportunity
To romanticize your existence
Because when the time comes
You will be reminiscing
On all the leaps you took
To satisfy your way of living
Without any regrets
In the back of your mind

I am done crediting others
For the devotion I have put
Into accomplishing my dreams

Untold Truths

Once you confront your fears
You will realize
Beyond the wall you built
Is the entirety
Of what the world has to offer

Intimacy is much more
Than locked lips
And tangled bodies

Intimacy is peeling
The layers off someone
Hoping to unveil
Every facet of them

Untold Truths

Allow your lover to dive into
The deepest parts of your soul
Let them carve
Through the hidden beauty
You have dimmed
All because you believed
Your spark was not enough

Anxiety is when
My consciousness disregards
The very feelings
That make me human
Making my thoughts constantly race
Compelling me into believing
A mirage fabricated by my own mind

You are corrupting
Your brain with negativity
By speaking to yourself
With such meanness
Instead fill your mind with kindness
And see how in tune you will be
With your body and mind

To be broken
Does not undermine
The perception of
What love encompasses

Hold me tighter
I feel at ease when you wrap
Your arms around me
With my face buried
In the crook of your neck
It is a place where I know
No harm can be done

Your arms are a safe haven
They are a quiet place
I know I can run into
When life gets too loud

I hope that one day
You will allow yourself
To let in someone
Who lets you
Express yourself
In healthy ways

The sun and the moon
Are in complete harmony
They are mindful
That when one is called upon
Watching the creation of the other
Is important in working hand in hand
So one does not outshine the other

Those doubts you keep having
Because you are scared
You will not succeed in life
Are the same reasons
To keep walking your path

Your racing thoughts
That evoke stress
Are nothing more
Than make-believe

I knew he was the one
When we would analyze
The poems that I would
Pour my heart into writing
He would let me read them
And slowly dissect the sentences
That I had created
Carefully listening
As I explained
What each line meant
He knew the value
Of the words being formed
Into meaningful sentences
I knew he was the one
When I spent countless hours
Working on this book
And he was by my side

You will find your highest self
In the palm of your hands
If you detach yourself
From pessimism

I wondered why
I wasn't deserving
Of a mother's love
Why I couldn't get
The kisses and hugs
Or the I love you
Why did I have to grow
Into the woman I am
Without one of
The most crucial
Forms of love

The moon
Is a heavenly body
Embellishing the starry sky
Displaying that in spite of
A sullen frame of mind
A dainty glow transcends
Regardless of predicament

Unfortunately
Humans search
For the love
They did not
Receive growing up
In unkind people
Even if that means
Being put through hell
Over and over again
Until they are
Loved by the
Right one

Nature is the one being
Where anguish *is not* present
Where tranquility *is not* disturbed
It encompasses the beauty in life
And when surrounded by greenery
Serenity begins to fill the mind
Establishing eternal bliss

Part 1

My greatest enemy
Has always been my body
Believing my physical appearance
Dictated who I was as a person
I'd look in the mirror
And be disgusted with what I saw
I'd point out everything wrong
With my figure
Every imperfection that I spotted
Even though those flaws
Were the finest aspects of me
My body should have been
My greatest prize
And not my greatest enemy

Part 2

I should have looked
At myself in the mirror
And smiled over the way I appeared
I should have pointed out
Everything flattering about my body
I should have pointed out
Every beautiful
And precious thing about myself
I needed to love my body
For what it was
Rather than putting myself down
For what I thought it should look like
It's so easy to overlook
All the positive aspects of your body
Yet embracing yourself
Is the most powerful reward

Angelina Mateus

I bathe in literature
Not to be wiser
But to escape
From my reality
Into another one
In hopes to temporarily
Forget about actuality
For just one moment

Falling in love
Is not the same as
Being in love

Why would you want to fall in love
When falling things tend to break

Would you not prefer to be in love
Where a deep-rooted connection forms

Parents are supposed to be
The primary definition of love
Mine showed me
The ugliest parts of it
Now I am slowly unlearning
The love that was taught to me
So that I can love
My partner with pureness

I grew up with expectations imposed
From loved ones
Their feelings
And view of me
Would factor into every decision
In hopes that I'd please them
When ideally
I should be freely living for myself

Before telling yourself
You are incapable
Of accomplishing what seems
Like the impossible
Think back on all the times
You prospered despite
Those words nagging
In the back of your mind

Healing
That's important
Taking the time to recover
From your heart being hurt
Maybe one too many times
Look forward and not backward
Each day is going to get better
Whether you see it or not
Some days
Are going to be harder than others
Some days
You'll either smile less or smile more
Just know you deserve happiness
Let your heart recover
Fully this time

I cannot wrap my head
Around the fact
That you left me motherless
All for your own benefit
What possessed you to leave a child
To explore the world of womanhood
Without a mother by their side
Guiding them in the direction needed
How could you

Even though the storm persisted
In pulling you underwater
Your resilience empowered
You to keep swimming to the surface
To take a moment to breathe
And find your way back home

Once I realized
I never needed you
It was easier to find love
Within myself

Solitude is not
Something you want to endure
But sadly
Many people do
People feel isolated
No matter what they have
Or who is in their lives
Solitude is not
A pleasant feeling
Not one bit

When you seek validation
In the wrong places
You don't realize the empty promises
Or the dishonesty escaping their lips
Forgetting about your morality
You allow yourself to find comfort
In a false reality
Fabricated by untruthful words

There will always be
People you mistake as significant

If you pay close attention
You will realize
They are not what they appear to be

The aching you feel
When you discover
The person you thought
Was remarkable
Is now the reason
Behind your affliction

What is truly heartbreaking
Is having the woman
Who was supposed to be
The mother figure I never had
Completely disregard
The motherly needs
My heart screamt for

I want it to be you
Because despite all the bad
Loving me unconditionally
Was all that you did
You soothed my racing thoughts
And kissed my insecurities away
You never tried to change me
You loved me as I was

Time and again it is said
Two broken people
Cannot form an attachment
Because in the end
The love will only
Break them more

Why is it
This type of love
Is viewed as destructive
When it is two souls
Aching for solicitude

Why does my house
Not feel like home
A home has
Walls
Windows
And rooms
Questions keep soaring
Why does home feel like you
A human being
With a pulsating heart
My stomach fluttering
At the sight of you
Your smile brightening up
The entire room
You possess the ability
To make the world
That surrounds us disappear
My heart is so incredibly fond of you
I can't comprehend how home can be you

Untold Truths

I kept wondering
Why you weren't loving me
But the truth is you were
In ways I never understood
Nor felt
I thought love consisted of
Gifts and physical touch
But love is so much more
Love is raw
It consists of wiping my tears away
Soothing me when anxiety sets in
Caressing me when I doubt
You taught me love comes
In a variety of shapes

You seek acceptance
From the same man who broke you
Because he gives you false hope
Making you promises
He cannot fulfill
Your heart still aches
For a man you don't even recognize
Lingering on someone
Who doesn't value you
Someone who continuously lies
And manipulates your feelings
Knowing he will not change
You stay by his side
All because you are too familiar
With his *"love"*

Untold Truths

Intertwined with webs
From your sticky threads
I hold my tongue
Silently listening
To your venomous notion
In hopes to be unbound
From your twisted sound

My father was 20 years young
Overcoming the obstacles
That accompanied
Being a single parent
I could never criticize him
For using the only tools
He knew to parent me with

I vow
To keep spreading
My wings
And to never let
Anyone else
Make me believe
I am not enough

I always doubted
The way you viewed me
However
My imperfections
Were your favourite parts of me

Blooming into something you desire
Takes time
Rain and sunshine
Are needed to form
Something beautiful
Happiness requires tears
As well as smiles
It will take time but you will succeed
You will flourish into
The idyllic version of yourself

My childhood
Was one small moment of my life
Where happiness was supposed
To be provided
Instead it was taken away
On multiple occasions
In response
To the misery in the lives of others

How can you let yourself
Believe your body
Is your worst enemy
When its purpose
Is supporting your very existence

Part 1

My innocence was ripped away
From me at a young age
The purity I had
Gone in a blink of an eye
He did that
He made me feel the way I do
The images flooding
Through my brain
When I least expect it
I should be mad at what he did to me
But the weird thing is
I'm not
I'm sad and I feel numb
I remember what he did to me
When I was just a few years old
His hands on just a little kid

Part 2

Growing up feeling
Disgusted with yourself
Blaming yourself for what he did
The truth is
I should not be held accountable
For his gruesome actions
I learnt to forgive but not to forget
Unfortunately things do happen
To good-hearted people
Reminiscing on the memories
You once shared with them
You start to wonder why you
What prompted you
To let yourself hurt this little girl

Part 3

Now you say
That was never your purpose
But God knows you still did it
I should have told you
I forgave you
Before you went to heaven
But why would you go to heaven
After your bad intentions
Beyond that you were closer to me
Than you ever intended
I'm sorry you died thinking
I didn't love you
Because I did
Despite the hell you put me through

Self-love is not selfish
Devoting time to yourself
Is not greedy
Taking care of your
Body
Mind
And soul
Is not foolish
Start choosing yourself

I lost myself in the promises
You repeatedly made

In hopes that perhaps
They would be of importance

The idea of love
Is not what frightens me
It is handing over my heart
To someone who has
No desire to protect it

What frightens me
Is having my heart handled
By someone who does not
Seek to display it to the world

My heart is meant
To be held by someone
Who will gracefully showcase
The intensity of our love

My body is different now
It is not the same one
You last touched

Do not stop healing
Think of how your soul will feel
When you finally free yourself
From the trauma
Your younger self endured

I poke at my body
And cover my blemishes
Taking a glance in the mirror
A little girl appears
Gleaming with delight

I feel a flicker of despair
Trying to grasp
How I could ridicule
My flourishing self
How I can deprecate
My prospering body
I couldn't possibly allow myself
To speak to little me
In the manner I do now

How could I be so cruel
To the very body
That has endured immensely

I am gradually learning
How to let you
Touch the parts of me
I always try to keep
Your hands away from

With complete regard
For my feelings
You softly plant kisses
On those parts of my body
Showing me you find me beautiful

Is it not crazy
How my insecurities
Are another man's treasure

The moon gleaming
The sun brightly beaming
The twinkling stars
The waves cascading on the cliffs
Flowers fluttering in the breeze
Oh how nature is magnificent

Value the seemingly little moments
That make you feel fulfilled

When you look in the mirror
Do not start insulting yourself
Because of formed insecurities
Instead admire
Who you have become
With repeated words of affirmation

You are strong
Is for the woman
I have grown to be
Even when the universe
Decided to throw
Shit my way

I will keep being strong
Is for continuing to stride
In the right direction
Regardless of the obstacles
That may ascend

You trail your hands on her body
With an inhuman craving
To satisfy your needs
No was not the word
You were looking for
Anger consuming you
You say she is pathetic and foolish
No man has ever belittled her
Taunted her
Made her feel any less of a human
But you do not care
Her body is all you seek
You don't yearn for love or affection
You lust for her
Lips
Hips
And curves
Yet you cannot have her
She is more
Than what you think she is
You are a coward
For believing a phenomenon
That creates life
Can ever want a lowlife like you

She creates life
She creates the sun and the moon
The waves and the mountains
The air you breathe
The path you walk on
All created by her beautiful soul

I am envious of my siblings
Saddened by the love
They both receive
With the collected
And emotionally available
Version of my father
My inner child is screaming
Wishing that patience came first
When he experienced distress
Wishing that he cared for me
In the ways that he cares for them
It comes noticed that
He undoubtedly loves me
Yet little me longs for the benignity
That my father is now providing

We have been told
Crying is a weakness
Or not to let emotions
Get the better of you
I say that is for people
Who are too weak
To express themselves

Certain situations
Are meant to be felt
Do yourself a favour
Let your emotions
Free themselves

Emotion is being human

.

There is someone in particular
An individual you long for
Giving you a sense
That there is no one else
All because they leave you
Feeling astounded

Your touch
Is a comfort
I never knew
I would crave

I want to help you heal
The parts of yourself
You have concealed
Because you believed
They could never
Be at peace again

Allow your heart to feel
The feeling of love
Engulf yourself
In the ecstasy that surges
When your soul undergoes passion

Your soul craves
The affection of another human
Your body lingers
For the touch of one's hands
Your mind wanting
Words of certainty
These feelings aren't soaring out
Because of multitudes
They're soaring out
Because of one person in particular

I get lost in the specks of your eyes
They are far more captivating
Than the stars in the sky

Part 1

Toxicity is defined as someone who
One minute is showering you
With words so beautiful
You feel warmth radiating
Through your entire body
Then the next
They're injecting you
With lethal doses of harmful words
Every unpleasant word
Filling you up like poison
It goes straight to your heart
Shattering a piece of it

Part 2

A routine starts to form
A cycle that can't seem to be broken
Knowing the damage they've caused
An attachment still begins to form
Intertwining with a dark soul
You can't seem
To detach yourself from
No matter how intense
Your anguish is
And it grows shallower every day
These wounds are not healing
All because you cannot let go

The kindness
You gracefully hand out
To those around you
Is the same kindness
Your heart is meant to feel

If you recombine
A mirror's shattered glass
Reflections do not vanish
Through the cracks
Take a close look in the mirror
Noticing the beauty
That lies within you

Protect your body
As it is the vessel
Carrying you through life

Untold Truths

You can depend on yourself
To wipe your tears away
And pick yourself back up
You are your own hero
Until the very end

The bare minimum
Does not align
With the person
I have grown to be
Aiming for the stars
Is the path
I am walking

A woman's figure is not a toy
Her body is not yours to touch
She is not meant to please you

Angelina Mateus

I simply wish you
Desired to stay a while longer
Before you became a foreigner

Untold Truths

You create excuses
And push away the dim view
That keeps resurfacing
With the purpose
That the legitimate truth
Will bide far away

Petals fall off of a flower
Because they are no longer needed

I need to detach myself from you
Because I am no longer needed

She is seeking sincerity
In the mirror that stands in her room
But cannot seem to believe
What the mirror presents to her
A mirror cannot lie

You were placed on this earth
With the intention
That you sculpt your own destiny
Do not let the wrong crowd
Change the route
You designed for yourself

If you will not help
Water the roots of my flower
Do not interrupt the time
Being put into ensuring
The flower blossoms
As intended

When you did the unimaginable
By taking my innocence
I was frightened of being used

How can I trust a man
To trail his hands on my body
When there is a never-ending battle
With my perception of intimacy

You spit out nonsense
Thinking you can tear me down
Without realizing
I am not the same little girl
Who soaked up
The detrimental words
Thrown her way

Attempting to hurt me
Shows you are projecting
Your insecurities onto me
In hopes of making me feel small
In comparison to you

Honey
I am better than you
Considering I do not walk
All over those I am meant to lift up

Being alone does not mean
You cannot allow yourself to flow
With the stillness of your presence

Do not be ashamed
Of celebrating your achievements
Announce to the world
All you have accomplished
You are worth celebrating

Part 1

People feel being young
Entails a lack of understanding
Of the world
That isn't the case at all
Children are more
Intelligent than you think
They have aspirations
You cannot fathom
Little me's desire
Is an illustration of that
Growing up
Without a biological mother
Prompted me
To want children of my own
To love them wholeheartedly

Part 2

People told me I was too young
Or that the impression
Would fade as I got older
But that feeling never came
My mother didn't want me
Yet this has made me
Want to become one
Having children of my own
And watching them grow up
Is something I yearn for

I lost myself in a world
Filled with unrealistic standards
Making me question
Who am I truly

There is one person
I wish would take the steps
In understanding me
Understand the years spent
Carrying responsibilities
That were not mine to hold

I want them to apologize
For the times I was mistreated
Considering all I have done
To ease the burdens of their world

I will forgive you

Lying down in your bed
Wrapped in your arms
With my cheek
Against your chest
You gently brush
Your fingertips on my skin
With no malicious intent
Just fondness radiating
When the delicacy
Of your hands caress
The body you swore
To shield from harm

I may be the poet
But you are the muse
I cannot afford to lose
Because our story
Permits me to write
About the type of love
Everyone daydreams about

I want to thank
All the women in my life
Who were selfless
And showed me
The ways of being a woman

These women
Could have turned away
From little me
As I was not their daughter
Yet they each took on an active role
In holding me tightly
Showing me nothing but kindness

I have nothing but appreciation
For the women
Who held out their hands
For me to hold onto
Until I was ready
To become the woman I am today

Delicately handled
At the core of a temple
An ethereal sculpture
Is sheltered from harm
Guarded from destruction
Symbolizing more than entity
A divine being glares down
Recognizing their significance

Stretch marks tell the story
Of how your body evolved
Into the shape you were intended for
When you look at them
Picture your body
Being surrounded
By tiny constellations
Revealing that you are a star

When life gets too dark
Look up
At the moon's illumination
And allow its energy
To flow through you

Doing so
A glow will transform
Inside your entity
Lighting up the dark segments
You have been trying to mend

The moon is speaking to you
By brightening the pieces
You need to heal
To permanently be whole again

As a child
I combed the beach
For broken seashells
With the analogy
That just because it's broken
Doesn't mean it isn't beautiful

Untold Truths

I doubted myself writing this book
Thinking I was too young
To have my name out in the world
Believing I would outgrow
The events and feelings
Written across these pages

I now recognize
My truth is forever a part of me
It will just be history
Stored in pages
Waiting to be read again

Manufactured by Amazon.ca
Bolton, ON

36030127R00061